FOODS OF THE WORLD

360 DEGREES, an imprint of Tiger Tales
5 River Road, Suite 128, Wilton, CT 06897
Published in the United States 2018
Originally published in Great Britain 2018 by Caterpillar Books
Text by Libby Walden • Text copyright © 2018 Caterpillar Books
Illustrations copyright © 2018 Jocelyn Kao
ISBN-13: 978-1-944530-20-4 • ISBN-10: 1-944530-20-7
Printed in China • CPB/1800/0865/0218

For more insight and activities, visit us at www.tigertalesbooks.com

FOODS OF THE WORLD

by Libby Walden • Illustrated by Jocelyn Kao

INTRODUCTION

We eat in order to fuel our bodies, but what we put on our plates can also be something with which to experiment and explore. We use food to offer comfort, show affection, or in celebration just as much as we use it to keep us going!

Availability of ingredients, styles, and traditions all influence what we eat, and although we need food to survive, our approach to it changes depending on where we are in the world. This book takes an in-depth tour of some of the traditions, trends, and tastes from around the globe.

CONTENTS

Section 1: Customs and Traditions 7

From Field to Plate — 8
Cooking with Fire — 10
La Gastronomie — 12
Fast Food! — 14
Unique Utensils — 16
Rude Food — 18
Unusual Tastes — 20
Health Warning! — 22
You Are What You Eat — 24
Super Foods! — 26
Swapping Plates — 28
Perfect Pastries — 30
Fascinating Food Facts — 32

Section 2: Playing with Food 33

Competitive Eating — 34
Forever Blowing Bubbles — 36

Food Fight! — 38
Digging For Buried Treasure — 40
Chocolate Coins — 42
To Dye For — 44
And Then There Was Light — 46
Fascinating Food Facts II — 48

Section 3: Celebrating Food 49

Eggs Will Roll — 50
Addressing the Haggis — 52
Plating Up Tradition — 54
Sunrise, Mooncake — 56
Fasting and Feasting — 58
Happy Birthday! — 60
Springtime Pancakes — 62

Poutine from Canada

Paella from Spain

Cocoa from Ecuador

Curry from India

Canada

Spain

India

Ecuador

CUSTOMS AND TRADITIONS

People around the world connect with their cultural or ethnic backgrounds through what they eat, even if they find themselves far away from home.

Food can tie us to our personal history, family, or country. In this section, we look at the ways different cultures approach and appreciate food.

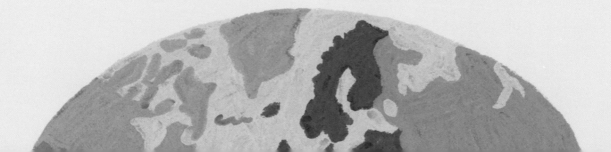

7

FROM FIELD TO PLATE

Farming is a global industry, with more than a third of the world's working population employed in agriculture. Countries harness the power of their climate, land, and soil to grow crops, fruit, and vegetables for themselves and to export to other countries around the world.

Maize is the most popular crop grown worldwide, followed by sugarcane. While both of these crops have other uses, the third most popular crop—rice—is grown solely for human consumption.

Paddy-field farming is the most common way to grow rice. Fields are flooded to give the semi-aquatic crop the best chance of survival. Paddy fields are common sights in the major rice-producing countries of China, India, Indonesia, and Vietnam.

COOKING WITH FIRE

There are hundreds of cooking techniques, from boiling or roasting to steaming or frying, but here are three ways chefs use fire to heat up the kitchen.

A *tandoor* is a fire-fueled circular clay or metal oven traditionally used in Indian cuisine. Tandoor chefs use this specialized oven to slowly cook skewered meat and to evenly bake flatbreads by pressing the dough against the sides of the oven.

Flambé is the French cooking method meaning "to flame"! This involves adding alcohol to a dish and then setting fire to it. The heat burns off the alcoholic content but keeps the flavor in the dish.

Whether you call it a barbecue (UK), a barbie (Australia), a cook-out (U.S.), a *braai* (South Africa), or an *al ha'esh* (Israel), the simple act of cooking food outdoors over an open flame is popular across the globe!

French cuisine is now so important that it was added to the U.N.E.S.C.O. list of the world's intangible cultural heritage to ensure its preservation.

LA GASTRONOMIE

Cuisine, restaurant, café, gastronomy (or gastronomie), haute cuisine, sauté, purée, julienne, menu—all of these words are common food terms that are used every day, and they all come from the French language.

The French have been pioneers of the food industry since the 17th century, when chefs, like François Pierre de la Varenne, reclaimed French cuisine from the influence of the Italians. La Varenne wrote the first French cookbook, *Le Cuisinier François*, in 1651, in which he established the early "rules" of French cooking.

By the 20th century, France was celebrated for its exquisite dishes. French chefs such as Marie-Antoine Carême and Georges Auguste Escoffier had become world-famous and helped France to become a modern gastronomic giant.

FAST FOOD!

Take-out delivery drivers are a common sight on many roads, but it seems that no one can compete with the efficiency of the Mumbai *dabbawalas*!

Established in the 19th century, *dabbawalas* collect approximately 200,000 home-cooked meals from family homes and deliver them to office workers across Mumbai every day. Each meal is labeled and color-coded to ensure the correct meal is delivered to the right person.

With just one mistake estimated per six million deliveries, the self-employed *dabbawalas* are the masters of Mumbai lunchtime!

MUMBAI CENTRAL

The special stacked lunch boxes are called tiffin boxes.

UNIQUE UTENSILS

Some cultures still eat using their hands, but most have developed specialized utensils with which to eat food and keep fingers clean!

Knives have been used as both a weapon and a utensil since prehistoric times.

The word fork comes from the Latin *furca*, meaning "pitchfork." Food is lifted or speared using the fork tines or prongs.

Used for eating liquid or semi-liquid foods, spoons come in a variety of materials—from wood to steel.

Designed to pick up food with a pincer movement, chopsticks are the main utensil of East Asia.

Can you guess what these unusual kitchen utensils are and what they might be used for? Answers can be found at the bottom of the page.

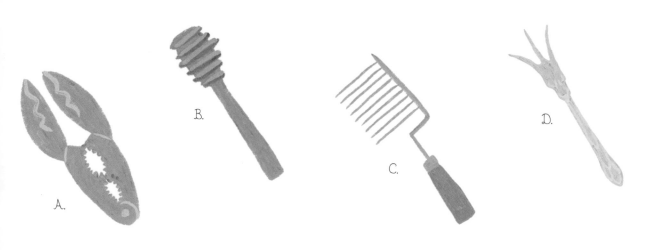

A. A crab cracker—used to break crab shells

B. A honey dipper—designed to drizzle honey without making a mess

C. A cake breaker—used to cut delicate sponge cakes

D. A lemon fork—the splayed tines expertly grip the curved citrus rind

RUDE FOOD

There are many different customs and rules related to eating around the world, which means that there are also many different ways to offend at the dining table....

In Thailand it is considered rude to stab your food with a fork as forks should only be used to push food onto your spoon.

───────────

While in many countries clearing your plate is considered good manners, in China, finishing your meal is seen as criticizing your host for not feeding you enough!

It is common in many Middle Eastern countries to eat with your fingers, but make sure you choose the correct hand! The left hand is traditionally used for wiping yourself after going to the toilet, and so, unsurprisingly, it is viewed as unclean to use the left hand at the dinner table!

UNUSUAL TASTES

These delicacies from around the world might not be to everyone's taste.

Fried tarantula (Cambodia)

A delicacy of the Cambodian town Skuon, the tarantulas are flavored with garlic, salt, and sugar, then deep fried to make this crunchy snack.

Hákarl (Iceland)

This Icelandic delicacy is actually decomposed shark meat. Buried underground in a shallow pit for several months, *hákarl* is then cut into strips and hung to dry before being served.

Century egg (China)

Also called *pidan*, this unusual snack is considered worth waiting for! Preserved for a few months, these eggs, when ready, will have a dark green yolk and the albumen (egg white) will be brown.

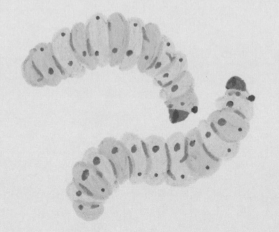

Witchetty grub (Australia)

Traditional food of the indigenous Australians, witchetty grubs are the large white larvae of the wood-eating moth. Viewed as a high-protein snack, they can be eaten raw or lightly baked.

Because of its poisonous properties, fugu is the only food the Emperor of Japan is forbidden to eat!

HEALTH WARNING!

Some people like to invite a little bit of danger to dinner, but none more so than the Japanese....

Fugu, or pufferfish, can be so deadly to diners that chefs have to undergo an extensive three-year training course just to be allowed to prepare it!

The liver and other inner organs of the *fugu* contain deadly amounts of the poison tetrodotoxin, which has no known antidote. This means the fish has to be *very* carefully prepared in order to be safe to eat.

YOU ARE WHAT YOU EAT

National dishes are recipes or foods that are strongly associated with a country's culture. Can you guess where these popular dishes are from?

A. There are more than 350 different types of pasta. It is a staple ingredient in many dishes found in this country.

B. A tagine is a dish named after the earthenware pot in which it is cooked. Tagines are slow-cooked, savory stews.

C. Typically eaten on a Sunday, roast dinner is often accompanied by stuffing, vegetables, and gravy.

D. Served over a small portable stove, fondue is a communal meal where bread is dipped into melted cheese using long-handled forks.

E. Peking duck is an ancient dish traditionally served with sliced spring onion, cucumber, and a sweet bean sauce, then wrapped in a thin pancake.

F. The term "hamburger" comes from the Hamburg steaks used in the creation of this dish, which German immigrants introduced to this particular country.

Answers: A. Italy, B. Morocco, C. England, D. Switzerland, E. China, F. United States

25

SUPER FOODS!

Some foods are better for us than others, and regularly eating fruit and vegetables is proven to be beneficial to our health. These colorful foods contain vitamins, minerals, and fiber that are key to staying healthy.

The nutrients in fruit and vegetables reduce the risk of colds and disease by helping the body to create more red blood cells and build a strong immune system. Variety is the spice of life, so eating a rainbow of fruit and vegetables will keep you strong and super-healthy!

SWAPPING PLATES

As more people travel and try new foods, the boundaries of cultural cooking can blur. For example, if you went to Greece on your vacation and loved the *dolmades* (stuffed vine leaves), you might try to cook them when you come home and share the recipe with your friends.

The food of South Africa is known as "rainbow cuisine" because it takes ingredients and influences from the many different cultures that have settled and continue to thrive in South Africa. There are 11 official languages of South Africa, so it's hardly surprising that the dishes found in the area are as diverse as its citizens.

Spices and curries have been adopted from Malay and Indian settlers.

Sausages, pies, and other meat-based dishes were introduced by the Dutch.

Maize, rice, and goat-meat dishes were staple foods of the indigenous tribes.

PERFECT PASTRIES

Sitting in bakery windows across the globe are appetizing, sugar-covered cakes and pastries designed to tempt and delight. Here are a few of the different sweet treats that you might find.

Baklava is a rich, sticky treat that is served in a bite-sized portion. To make this dish, filo pastry is layered with nuts and then sweetened with honey or syrup.

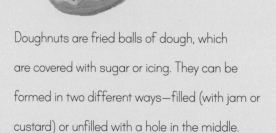

Doughnuts are fried balls of dough, which are covered with sugar or icing. They can be formed in two different ways—filled (with jam or custard) or unfilled with a hole in the middle.

Traditionally served at French or Italian weddings, the *croquembouche* (translated as "crunches in the mouth") is a decorated tower made from choux pastry profiteroles, bound together by spun sugar.

Strudel, a filled and crisp pastry dessert, is a famous Austrian dish. Traditional pastry chefs say that the pastry used for strudel should be thin enough to read a newspaper through.

Originating from Sicily, *cannoli* are tube-shaped shells of fried pastry with a sweet filling. Flavors range from plain ricotta to orange to chocolate, and they come in all sizes!

FASCINATING FOOD FACTS

There are many phobias related to food but arachibutyrophobia is the word given to the fear of having peanut butter stuck to the roof of your mouth!

The shape of a pretzel is supposed to represent arms crossed in prayer. According to legend, pretzels were invented by an Italian monk who would give folded strips of bread dough to children as a *pretiola* (little reward) for their prayers.

PLAYING WITH FOOD

As children, we are usually told not to play with our food, but of course, food can be great fun! From enormous village food fights to coloring our clothes, what we eat can be so much more than what we put on our plates.

COMPETITIVE EATING

Popular in Japan, Canada, and the United States, eating competitions are often held at local fairs, but there are also professional contests.

Participants, amateur and professional, have to eat as much of a certain type of food as they can within a specific amount of time in order to win glory, a trophy, or a cash prize.

Typical foods include hamburgers, hot dogs, and chicken wings, although some more obscure foods have been used to challenge the strongest of stomachs—cheese curds, whole turkeys, or oysters, anyone?

FOREVER BLOWING BUBBLES

Chewing gum is an unusual "food" because although it requires the act of chewing, it offers no nutritional value as it should never be swallowed!

It is a culinary habit that dates back to early civilization. The Ancient Greeks and Mayans used to chew tree resin as a way to reduce hunger pangs and freshen their breath, but it wasn't until the 19th century that gum became the commercial product that it is today.

Bubble gum, however, was created completely by accident! In the 1920s, Walter Diemer, an accountant for the Fleer Chewing Gum Company, was experimenting with new gum recipes when he unintentionally created a new type of gum. It was less sticky than normal chewing gum, but it was stretchier—so stretchy, in fact, that you could blow bubbles with it!

FOOD FIGHT!

Food fights are often impromptu battles where whatever food is available is launched at "the enemy." Some food fights, such as the annual tomato fight of Buñol, Spain, have now become a part of culture and tradition.

The *battaglia delle arance* is the largest food fight in Italy. Every February, the city of Ivera becomes a battleground, as nine groups of "foot soldiers" attack the horse-drawn "king's guards" with oranges.

The three-day event commemorates the rebellion of the townspeople against the tyrannical lords who ruled Ivera in the Middle Ages. The festival is closed with a silent march and a farewell from the appointed "General."

DIGGING FOR BURIED TREASURE

Truffles are one of the oldest and most expensive food ingredients on the planet. As they grow underground in wooded areas, truffles require skilled, albeit unusual, hunters to find the black or white gold.

Trained truffle hogs have helped people "hunt" truffles since Roman times. These ancient foragers have an excellent sense of smell and can find truffles buried 3 feet (1 m) underground!

CHOCOLATE COINS

Chocolate was originally the secret of ancient Central America and a delicacy of both the Mayan and Aztec diet. Archaeological evidence tells us that the Mayans were drinking bitter, spiced chocolate as early as 1900 BC!

The Aztecs adopted the cacao bean from the Mayans, but there was a problem. Their home in the Mexican highlands was unsuitable for growing the cacao plant, so they had to find a way to import it.

The conquered Mayans were therefore required to pay the Aztecs tax or "tribute" in the form of the precious cacao beans, and because of this, cacao became a valuable form of currency within Aztec culture.

Cacao pods are grown...

then harvested...

and the beans are extracted...

and dried in the Sun...

then roasted...

crushed...

and pressed until...

raw chocolate is formed!

TO DYE FOR

Throughout history, people have been drawn to colorful clothing, and before synthetic dyes were invented in the 19th century, natural materials were gathered, stewed, and boiled to create dyes that were used to brighten up any wardrobe.

Vegetable dyes were particularly popular and roots, berries, fungi, and spices were also used to transform wools, silks, and cottons into colorful materials.

Expensive spices, such as turmeric, paprika, and saffron, were used to make vibrant orange-yellows.

Mushrooms were used to create earthier tones of yellow, brown, blue, and green.

Purple dyes were created from blackberries, boiled basil leaves, and elderberries.

Beetroots, madder herb roots, and rose hips were used to make varying shades of red.

AND THEN THERE WAS LIGHT

Most of us are familiar with the American art of pumpkin carving that takes place to celebrate Halloween, but did you know that the pumpkin is not the only vegetable that is used to create a lantern?

Taking place in November, *Räbechilbi* (or "turnip party") is a Swiss tradition where locals carve lanterns out of turnips. The largest celebration takes place outside of Zürich where, since 1905, the people of Richterswil have honored the humble turnip by organizing a town parade featuring more than 29 tons (26 tonnes) of the carved vegetable.

The turnip lanterns are supposed to represent the warmth of home during the cold winter months, and they are used to light up the elaborate parade floats as well as decorating the streets and houses of the town.

FASCINATING FOOD FACTS II

Feeling thirsty? Have a cucumber! Cucumbers are one of the most hydrating foods to eat, as they are 96% water.

The West African "miracle fruit" is a berry that, when eaten, is able to transform sour tastes (such as citrus fruits) to sweet.

Honey is the only natural food that can never rot—it can last 3,000 years without spoiling!

CELEBRATING FOOD

We often celebrate the most important events of our lives with food, or in turn, use food to mark a particular occasion or date.

For example, a cake is just a combination of flour, eggs, butter, and sugar until candles are put on top of it—then, for many, it becomes a birthday cake!

The White House Egg Roll is a race! Children use long-handled spoons to push their egg across the lawn.

START

START

START

EGGS WILL ROLL

Every spring, the Christian festival of Easter is celebrated. As well as special Easter church services, Christians exchange dyed, painted, marzipan, or chocolate eggs to symbolize the empty tomb from which it is believed Jesus was resurrected.

Children often participate in Easter-related activites, such as egg hunts and egg rolls. One of the more famous egg rolls takes place on the lawn in front of the White House and is hosted by the President and First Lady of the United States.

ADDRESSING THE HAGGIS

January 25 is an important date on the Scottish calendar. It is the day dedicated to the celebration of the famous Scottish poet Robert "Rabbie" Burns. The tradition of honoring Burns began in 1801 when Burns' friends first held a meal in his memory.

Burns Night celebrations tend to vary in size and decadence, but the evening is typically filled with speeches, poetry recitals, bagpipes, and the traditional Burns Night dinner of neeps (mashed swede), tatties (mashed potato), and haggis.

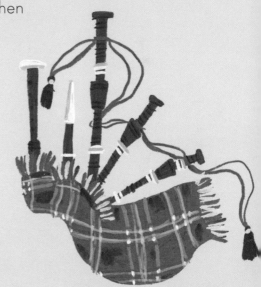

Haggis is a savory pudding made from the heart, lungs, and liver of a sheep mixed with onion, oatmeal, spices, and fat. It is then encased in a sheep's stomach and baked.

———————

This unusual dish is the centerpiece of the Burns Night dinner. The haggis is brought into the dining room to the sound of bagpipes. The host of the meal will then rise to recite Burns' poem "Address to a Haggis" before stabbing and toasting the dish. Only then will the haggis be served.

PLATING UP TRADITION

Every spring, the Jewish community celebrates *Pesach* (also known as Passover). This festival commemorates the Biblical story of Moses and how he freed the Israelite slaves from the Egyptian pharaoh, as told in Exodus.

A special feast is held on the first night of *Pesach*, known as the *Seder*. At the center of the meal is the Seder Plate, a special plate that contains symbolic foods that are significant to the retelling of Moses' story.

Maror (bitter herbs)
The bitter herbs or horseradish symbolize the bitterness of slavery.

Chazeret (bitter vegetable)
Endive or romaine lettuce is used to also symbolize the bitterness of slavery.

Beitzah (hard-boiled egg)

The egg represents the gifts that would have been brought to the Holy Temple.

Zeroah (lamb shank)

The bone is to symbolize the lamb that was sacrificed at the Holy Temple in ancient times.

פסח

Charoset (mix of apple, nuts, spices, and wine)

This represents bricks and mortar to remember the hard labor suffered by the slaves of Ancient Egypt.

Karpas (salted vegetables)

Parsley, onion, or potato dipped in salt water symbolizes the sweat and tears of Jewish slaves.

SUNRISE, MOONCAKE

The ancient Chinese observed that the movement of the Moon marked the changing of seasons, and more significantly, the arrival of the harvest. Every autumn, during a full Moon, they would give offerings to the Moon to say thank you, and this celebration continues in modern China today.

In Chinese culture, the full Moon symbolizes completeness and prosperity, and so the special cake of the modern Mid-Autumn festival is deliberately designed to complement the full harvest Moon.

Filled pastries known as mooncakes are shared with relatives during the festival to wish them a long and happy life. They come in different flavors and styles, but they are always round to reflect the shape of the Moon.

FASTING AND FEASTING

In Islamic culture, Ramadan marks the holy month of fasting, or *sawm*. It is a time when Muslims do not eat or drink anything during daylight hours. They rise before the Sun in the morning to eat and will only break their fast with a meal known as *Iftar* once the Sun has set.

Fasting during the month of Ramadan is one of the five pillars, or instructions, of Islam. The practice of *sawm* is designed to focus the mind and purify the body, ready for worship. It also reminds Muslims of those less fortunate than themselves.

The end of Ramadan is marked with the exchanging of gifts and a big communal celebration or feast, known as *Eid-ul-Fitr*.

HAPPY BIRTHDAY!

For many people around the world, a birthday is marked with a special birthday cake. The modern birthday cake tradition was first introduced in 15th-century Germany when bakeries began to sell single-tier cakes to their customers to celebrate. But cake is not the only way that people choose to mark the occasion.

In China, *shou tao* are common gifts for people on their birthday to wish them a long life. These lotus-paste-filled buns are designed to look like peaches, a fruit associated with immortality in Chinese culture.

A Mexican birthday party isn't complete unless there's a *piñata*! A hollow papier-mâché shape is filled with sweets and toys and then hung up, ready for blindfolded children to try to crack it open with a stick!

While birthday cakes are common in Russia, there are also special birthday pies. These fruit-filled pies are usually double-crusted and have the name of the birthday boy or girl written in pastry on the top.

SPRINGTIME PANCAKES

Maslenitsa is a popular Slavic festival that has roots in both pagan and Christian history. Celebrated just before the start of Christian Lent, Maslenitsa is a weeklong festival that marks the end of winter.

The signature food of the festival is the humble pancake, which is cooked in vast quantities and used in almost every aspect of the festivities. Pancakes are made every day, and they represent the Sun. By eating (a lot!) of pancakes, it is believed that festival-goers are consuming the warmth and energy of the Sun itself.

In Russian, the name of the festival derives from *maslo*, meaning butter or oil, which is why the festival is sometimes called butter week!